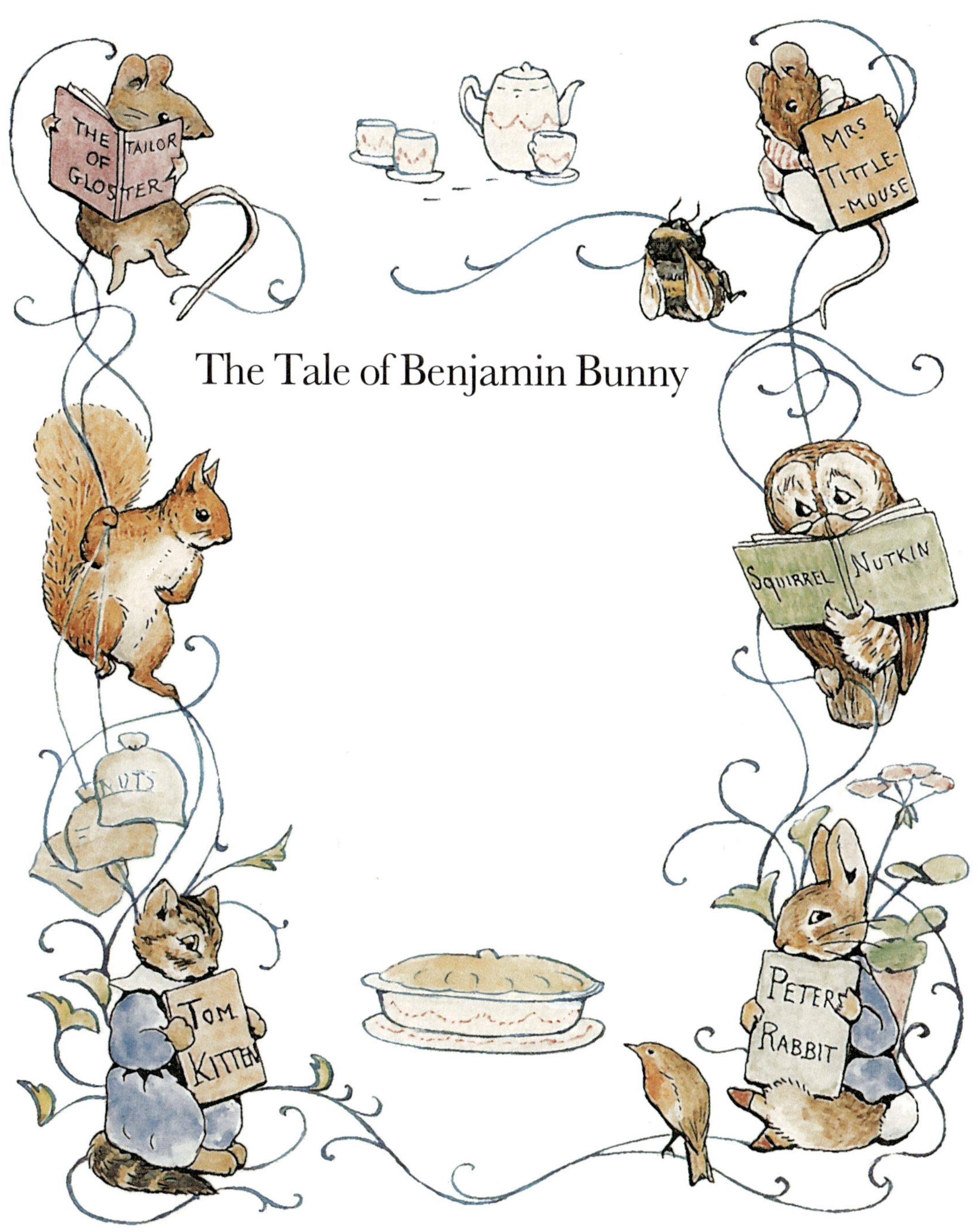

The Tale of Benjamin Bunny

The Tale of Benjamin Bunny

By Beatrix Potter

THE CLASSIC

One morning a little rabbit sat on a bank.

He pricked his ears and listened

to the trit-trot, trit-trot of a pony.

A gig was coming along the road; it was

driven by Mr. McGregor, and

beside him sat Mrs. McGregor

in her best bonnet.

As soon as they had passed,

little Benjamin Bunny slid down

into the road, and set off—with a hop,

skip, and a jump—to call upon his relations,

who lived in the wood at the back of

Mr. McGregor's garden.

TEA & Tobacco

That wood was full of rabbit holes;

and in the neatest, sandiest hole of all lived

Benjamin's aunt and his cousins—

Flopsy, Mopsy, Cotton-tail, and Peter.

Old Mrs. Rabbit was a widow;

she earned her living by knitting

rabbit-wool mittens and muffatees

(I once bought a pair at a bazaar).

She also sold herbs, and rosemary tea,

and rabbit-tobacco (which is what

we call lavender).

Josephine Bunny.
licensed to sell
TEA & TOBACCO

Little Benjamin did not very much

want to see his Aunt.

He came round the back of the fir-tree,

and nearly tumbled upon the top of

his Cousin Peter.

Peter was sitting by himself.

He looked poorly, and was dressed

in a red cotton pocket-handkerchief.

"Peter,"—said little Benjamin,

in a whisper—"who has got your clothes?"

Peter replied,—"The scarecrow

in Mr. McGregor's garden,"

and described how he had been

chased about the garden,

and had dropped his shoes and coat.

Little Benjamin sat down beside

his cousin, and assured him that

Mr. McGregor had gone out in a gig,

and Mrs. McGregor also;

and certainly for the day, because she

was wearing her best bonnet.

Peter said he hoped that it would rain.

At this point, old Mrs. Rabbit's voice

was heard inside the rabbit hole, Calling—

"Cotton-tail! Cotton-tail!

Fetch some more camomile!"

Peter said he thought he might feel better

if he went for a walk. They went away

hand in hand, and got upon the flat top

of the wall at the bottom of the wood.

From here they looked down into

Mr. McGregor's garden.

Peter's coat and shoes were plainly to be seen

upon the scarecrow, topped with an old

tam-o-shanter of Mr. McGregor's.

Little Benjamin said, "It spoils people's clothes to squeeze under a gate; the proper way to get in, is to limb down a pear tree."

Peter fell down head first; but it was of no consequence, as the bed below was newly raked and quite soft.

It had been sown with lettuces.

They left a great many odd little

foot-marks all over the bed,

especially little Benjamin,

who was wearing clogs.

Little Benjamin said that the first

thing to be done was to get back

Peter's clothes, in order that they might

be able to use the pocket-handkerchief.

They took them off the scarecrow.

There had been rain during the night;

there was water in the shoes,

and the coat was somewhat shrunk.

Benjamin tried on the tam-o-shanter,

but it was too big for him.

Then he suggested that they should fill

the pocket handkerchief with onions,

as a little present for his Aunt.

Peter did not seem to be enjoying himself;

he kept hearing noises.

Benjamin, on the contrary, was perfectly at home, and ate a lettuce leaf.

He said that he was in the habit of coming to the garden with his father to get lettuces for their Sunday dinner. (The name of little Benjamin's papa was old Mr. Benjamin Bunny.)

The lettuces certainly were very fine.

Peter did not eat anything;

he said he should like to go home.

Presently he dropped half the onions.

Little Benjamin said that it was not
possible to get back up the peartree
with a load of vegetables.

He led the way boldly towards
the other end of the garden.

They went along a little walk on planks,
under a sunny, red-brick wall.

The mice sat on their door-steps
cracking cherry-stones;
they winked at Peter Rabbit and
little Benjamin Bunny.

Presently Peter let the
pocket-handkerchief go again.

They got amongst flower-pots,

and frames, and tubs;

Peter heard noises worse than ever;

his eyes were as big as lolly-pops!

He was a step or two in front of his cousin,

when he suddenly stopped.

This is what those little rabbits

saw round that corner!

Little Benjamin took one look,

and then, in half a minute less than no time,

he hid himself and Peter and the onions

underneath a large basket....

The cat got up and stretched herself,

and came and sniffed at the basket.

Perhaps she liked the smell of onions!

Anyway, she sat down upon the

top of the basket.

She sat there for *five hours.*

I cannot draw you a picture of

Peter and Benjamin underneath the basket,

because it was quite dark,

and because the smell of onions was fearful;

it made Peter Rabbit and little Benjamin cry.

The sun got round behind the wood,

and it was quite late in the afternoon;

but still the cat sat upon the basket.

At length there was a pitter-patter,

pitter-patter, and some bits of mortar

fell from the wall abobe.

The cat looked up and saw

old Mr. Benjamin Bunny prancing along

the top of the wall of the upper terrace.

He was smoking a pipe of rabbit-tobacco,

and had a little switch in his hand.

He was looking for his son.

Old Mr. Bunny had no opinion

whatever of cats.

He took a tremendous jump off

the top of the wall on to he top of the cat,

and cuffed it off the basket,

and kicked it into the green-house,

scratching off a handful of fur.

The cat was too much surprised

to scratch back.

When old Mr. Bunny had driven

the cat into the green-house,

he locked the door.

When old Mr. Bunny had driven the cat

into the green-house, he locked the door.

Then he came back to the basket

and took out his son Benjamin by the ears,

and whipped him with the little switch.

Then he took out his nephew Peter.

Then he took out the handkerchief

of onions, and marched out of the garden.

When Mr. McGregor returned about half

an hour later he observed several

things which perplexed him.

It looked as though some person

had been walking all over the garden

in a pair of clogs—only the foot-marks

were too ridiculously little!

Also he could not understand how the cat

could have managed to shut herself up

inside the greenhouse,

locking the door upon the *outside*.

When Peter got home, his mother

forgave him, because she was so glad to

see that he had found his shoes and coat.

Cotton-tail and Peter folded up the

pocket-handkerchief, and old Mrs. Rabbit

strung up the onions and hung them

from the kitchen ceiling,

with the bunches of herbs

and the rabbit-tobacco.

The Tale of Benjamin Bunny
by Beatrix Potter

Published by The Classic Publishing Co.
ⓒ The Classic Publishing 2013
All rights reserved. No part of publication may be reproduced,
stored in a retrieval system, or transmitted, in any form or by any means,
without the permission of the copyright holder, The Classic Publishing Co.
Color art by The Classic Publishing Co.

The Classic in Mirbookcompany Publishing Co. Ltd.
239-18, Yeonnam-dong, Mapo-gu, Seoul, Korea
Telephone : 02-3141-4421 Fax : 02-3141-4428
Web site : cafe.naver.com/mirbookcompany
E-mail : sanhonjinju@naver.com